ESSENTIAL OILS

Guide Book

Learn about the uses of
essential oils.

INTRODUCTION

Welcome to the wonderful world of Essential Oils!

This kit is designed specifically for adults.

Learning a new skill is always exciting – we're here to help you get started. An essential oil diffuser can be used to freshen your home with vibrant scents, or you can use it for relaxation as well as to relieve stress, and lower anxiety. Essential oils are said to have many beneficial properties, and given that there are so many to choose from, you can have fun experimenting with the fragrances you prefer the most. Because essential oil diffusers are small, you also have the choice of where you would like to place them in your home.

Let's get your creativity flowing and open your mind to this new and unlimited world.

This kit provides everything you need to make your very own Essential Oil Diffuser. There is also an added option for you to try, complete with step-by-step instructions.

Remember, every skill takes a little time to learn. Experiment with the amount of oil you use until you are satisfied. The most important thing is that you have fun and enjoy yourself.

Let's start your Essential Oil Diffuser journey!

KIT CONTENTS

WHAT'S INCLUDED:

· 2x Hanging diffusing bottles
· 2x Essential oils 5ml (rose and lavender)

WHAT YOU'LL NEED:

· Reed diffuser (optional)
· Bergamot oil (optional)
· Peppermint oil (optional)
· Sweet Orange oil (optional)
· Lemongrass oil (optional)

Ingredients:
Lavender oil, Propylene glycol, Linalool acetate, linabol, Lavender oil
Rose oil, Propylene glycol, Phenyl ethanol, Rose alcohol, Citronellol, Naonanoate ethyl ester, Eugenol.

WHAT ARE ESSENTIAL OILS?

Essential oils are extracted from the flowers, seeds, leaves, stems, bark, or roots of plants. The oils are usually steam distilled or cold pressed. They are called essential because they contain the "quintessence" of the plant - the embodiment, or the essence.
Plants make these oils as part of their survival. They coat their leaves to protect against bacteria, fungi and viruses, as well as reducing drying out. The smells also attract pollinators and can repel browsers.

DO ESSENTIAL OILS WORK?

Some people are so convinced by the health benefits of essential oils, that they use nothing else for medicine, cleaning products or personal care. On the other hand, there are some who consider them "old wives' tales". But surely, you wouldn't use something time and again, if it didn't work? There have been over 200,000 clinical tests conducted on essential oils that tell us those old wives tales were not wrong.

HOW DO ESSENTIAL OIL DIFFUSERS WORK?

A diffuser basically breaks down the oil and water particles and distributes the particles into the air. This is called permeation. There are many types of diffusers, but the items in this kit are 'evaporative oil diffusers'. These are the easiest to set up and use.

FINDING THE BEST ESSENTIAL OILS FOR YOUR HOME:

Bedroom:
Essential oils are known for their relaxing qualities, so are ideal for the bedroom. Particularly beneficial are; lavender, mandarin, bergamot or ylang-ylang. All of these are known to help reduce stress and help you relax.

Living room:
The living room is where you can personalise your oils to your mood, the time of year or the weather. If you want something to invigorate you, then peppermint or a citrus scent can give you the lift you need. Similarly, if you're feeling congested or anxious, you can use eucalyptus or bergamot to help you decompress and decongest.

Bathroom:
This is the ideal place to use a reed diffuser. Not only do they look decorative, they also add a fresh and pleasant scent to your bathroom. It's an area where lemon grass or sweet orange would work well.

Kitchen:
Your kitchen can be inclined to hold cooking smells, so essential oils are perfect for breaking down toxins and neutralising fatty smells.

Top Tips
As with all oils, experiment until you find a scent you love, and don't be afraid to blend!

Remember, some oils are stronger than others and some people's smell is more sensitive than others, so a good starting point is 3 drops for the first time. We would not recommend anything more than 10 drops maximum per 10ml of water.

Playing around with different essential oils, diffusers, and locations can be really fun. It's important to consider the location of your diffuser. It needs to be placed on a flat, sturdy surface - below eye level is ideal. Avoid direct sunlight, and do not place anywhere near a strong draught, like near a fan. The diffuser is light and will easily blow over.

WARNINGS!

All the makes included in this book are designed specifically for adults.

Keep all ingredients and finished products out of the reach of children and pets.

Always dilute the essential before using. Avoid direct skin contact with undiluted oil as this may cause irritation. Do not ingest as may be fatal. If swallowed seek immediate medical attention. May cause an allergic skin reaction. Dispose of responsibly.
Harmful to aquatic life.

Not to be used with drugs that induce sleep. If taking medications, please consult your doctor before using any aromatherapy oils.

HANGING FRAGRANCE DIFFUSING BOTTLES

KIT CONTENTS

- 1x Lavender essential oil
- 1x Rose essential oil
- 2x Hanging diffusing bottles

METHOD

1. Prepare a clean, flat, nonporous surface (in case of any accidental spillages).

2. Unscrew the lid of the 8ml bottle and remove the rubber stopper.

3. Fill most of the bottle with warm tap water - it will help the oil to diffuse into a vapor.

4. Add 3 drops of your essential oil of choice. For a more intense fragrance drop up to 8 drops of essential oil. Now, screw the lid back onto the bottle.

5. Making sure the lid is tight, turn the bottle upside down for a few seconds.

6. The oil will slowly diffuse through the wooden lid of the bottle.

7. Place or hang your diffuser in a suitable room and safe area

REED DIFFUSER

1. Prepare a clean, flat, nonporous surface (in case of any accidental spillages).

2. Unscrew the chrome lid of the bottle.

3. Fill most of the bottle with oil tap water - it will help the water to diffuse into a vapour better.

4. Refer to the manufacturers instructions for safe and effective levels of oil to use in your diffuser.

5. Screw the lid back onto the bottle and add the wooden ring.

6. Place your reeds into the bottle – the oil will slowly diffuse through the reeds.

8. Place your diffuser in a safe area in the room of your choosing.

NOTES

Use the space below to make your own personal notes on essential oils.

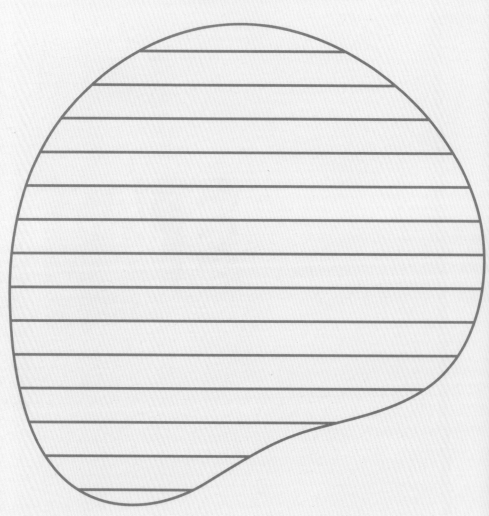

LAVENDER OIL

Lavender oil, also known by its scientific name Lavandula angustifolia, is a type of essential oil derived from the lavender flower.

BENEFITS OF LAVENDER

WHAT IT IS:

Lavender is a small aromatic evergreen shrub; it has narrow leaves and blue/purple flowers which are used in perfumery and medicine. The fragrant oil is extracted from the flowers through a process of distillation.

WHERE IT ORIGINATES FROM:

Originally from the Mediterranean, lavender is now grown across the world wherever there is sunshine, rain, and well-drained soil.

HEALTH BENEFITS:

Lavender oil is believed to have antiseptic and anti-inflammatory properties.

USES FOR LAVENDER

HEALING PROPERTIES:

Lavender oil is known to help reduce stress and anxiety, as well as relieve headaches. It can also help promote calmness and
restful sleep.

HOW TO USE:

Essential oils can be used in many ways; you can add a few drops onto a handkerchief or even your pillow cover. Alternatively, you can dilute a few drops with what's called a 'carrier or base' oil. Oils such as; coconut oil, olive oil, sweet almond oil, argan or avocado oil. You can also add a couple of drops to your daily/nightly moisturiser or body balm. Or, add to an essential oil diffuser to fragrance the room.

*If adding essential oil to any product that is intended for the skin, always read the manufacturers instructions, check the amount of essential oils that can be added to the product.

ROSE OIL

Rosa damascena is known for having many qualities in health and beauty but it's fragrance can also be beneficial. Rose scent can help target anxiety and depression as well as enhancing mood in general.

BENEFITS OF ROSE

WHAT IT IS:

Rose oil is an aromatic oil, usually extracted from rose petals. Rose oil has been used in natural beauty treatments, as well as addressing health conditions for hundreds of years. Commercial rose oil typically comes from the damask rose (Rosa damascena) plant. It can also be used as a natural perfume.

WHERE IT ORIGINATES FROM:

Rose oil comes originally from Bulgaria. The country produces rich and fragrant oil - it is the most expensive rose oil in the world.

HEALTH BENEFITS:

Antibacterial and anti-fungal properties.

USES FOR ROSE

HEALING PROPERTIES:

Traditionally, rose oil has been used to help promote calmness and wound healing and also helps to alleviate coughs, allergies and headaches. Being a great mood improver, it is good for targeting anxiety and depression. On top of this, it can also help fight acne and boost skin health with potential anti-aging benefits.

HOW TO USE:

To benefit from its wonderful floral scent, you can diffuse it in the air. Once you feel cofident with essential oils there are many ways to experiment with the fragrance.

BERGAMOT OIL

BENEFITS OF BERGAMOT

WHAT IT IS:

Bergamot is a citrus fruit plant. Bergamot is characterised by its aromatic scent, which is often described as floral and zesty. It features heavily in perfumes, soap-making, aromatherapy, and more.

WHERE IT ORIGINATES FROM:

The bergamot orange is a citrus fruit cultivated mainly in Italy. The tree has a yellow-green fruit, and the peel is valued for its flavouring.

HEALTH BENEFITS:

It has is antibacterial, antispasmodic and anti-inflammatory qualities.

USES FOR BERGAMOT

HEALING PROPERTIES:

It helps relieves anxiety and stress, regulates moods, helps manage digestive comfort, clears the airways, and cleanses the skin. It can have the added benefit of lifting your spirits, and generally promoting healing.

HOW TO USE:

Enjoy the fragrance from an essential oil diffuser or carry a few drops on a handkerchief in your pocket. You can also add a few drops to your body wash, shampoo, or face scrubs. It is an oil that can be sprayed, massaged in, bathed in, or diffused.

*If adding essential oil to any product that is intended for the skin, always read the manufacturers instructions, check the amount of essential oils that can be added to the product.

EUCALYPTUS OIL

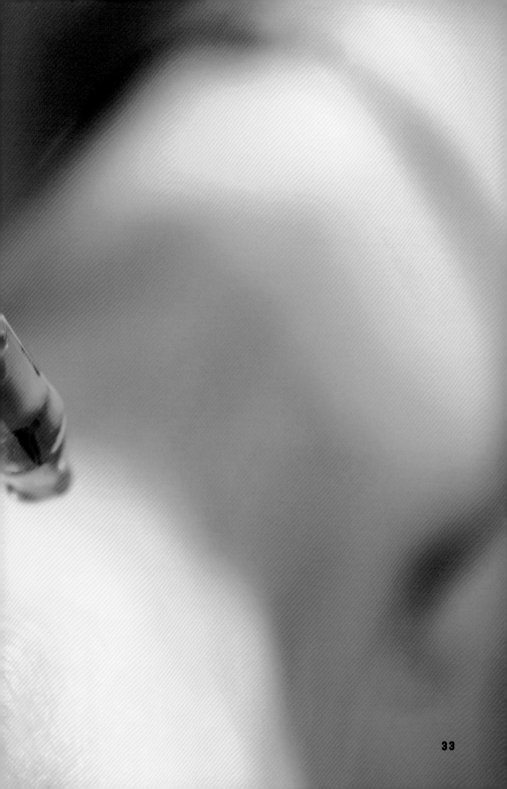

BENEFITS OF EUCALYPTUS

WHAT IT IS:

Eucalyptus oil is an aromatic, natural plant extract. The oil is derived from the leaves of the eucalyptus tree, and is a cleanser, purifier and revitaliser commonly used in aromatherapy, beauty products, and in traditional medicinal products.

WHERE IT ORIGINATES FROM:

The eucalyptus tree originates from Australia, but the essential oil can now be distilled from eucalyptus trees grown in various regions of the world, including Australia, South America, Africa and India.

HEALTH BENEFITS:

A natural disinfectant antiseptic, and offering some pain relief.

USES FOR EUCALYPTUS

HEALING PROPERTIES:

Helps you breathe easier, and is great for respiratory conditions. It also helps to keep bugs at bay.

HOW TO USE:

Enjoy the fragrance from an essential oil diffuser or carry a few drops on a handkerchief in your pocket. You can also mix it into a warm bath. It is an oil that can be sprayed, massaged in, bathed in or diffused.

*If using essential oil that is intended for the skin, always read the manufacturers instructions and check the amount of essential oils that can be used safely.

PEPPERMINT OIL

BENEFITS OF PEPPERMINT

WHAT IT IS:

The peppermint plant is classed as being a herb and is a mix of watermint and spearmint. Peppermint essential oil comes from both the flowers and leaves. The entire peppermint plant contains menthol, which provides a cooling sensation.

WHERE IT ORIGINATES FROM:

The peppermint plant grows throughout Europe and North America

HEALTH BENEFITS:

Peppermint oil has fantastic stomach settling properties

USES FOR PEPPERMINT

HEALING PROPERTIES:

Peppermint oil also helps relax muscles and can boost hair health.

HOW TO USE:

Peppermint oil can be used in so many ways. It can be applied topically to the skin using a carrier or base oil, such as jojoba oil. Or, you can pop some in a diffuser and breathe in the refreshingly minty scent all around you. You can also bathe in it, either on its own or combined with other complementary essential oils, such as lavender and geranium.

*If using essential oil that is intended for the skin, always read the manufacturers instructions and check the amount of essential oils that can be used safely.

SWEET
ORANGE OIL

BENEFITS OF SWEET ORANGE

WHAT IT IS:

Sweet orange essential oil is one of the most popular essential oils within aromatherapy. Unlike most essential oils that are extracted using steam distillation, most citrus oils, including sweet orange oil, are extracted by cold pressing the rinds of the orange. It has a sweet and citrus fragrance.

WHERE IT ORIGINATES FROM:

Originally from China, this evergreen tree has dark green leaves and white flowers, producing bright orange fruit.

HEALTH BENEFITS:

It holds antioxidant and antimicrobial qualities. It is said to be able to help with pain reduction, inflammation and can provide relief for stomach upset.

USES FOR SWEET ORANGE

HEALING PROPERTIES:

Sweet orange essential oil has be known to help with insommia. Promotes radience and smoothness of skin and mixed with lemon it can give you an uplifting energy boost.

HOW TO USE:

In a diffuser, or as a spray (diluted). It can also be steamed or used as a massage oil.

*If using essential oil that is intended for the skin, always read the manufacturers instructions and check the amount of essential oils that can be used safely.

LEMONGRASS OIL

BENEFITS OF LEMONGRASS

WHAT IT IS:

Lemongrass is a herb with a lemony scent. Its oil is extracted from the leaves of lemongrass plants, which usually involves steam distillation. The oil is extensively used in aromatherapy to revitalise the body.

WHERE IT ORIGINATES FROM:

Native to Africa, Asia and Australia, the lemongrass plant has long been thought of as a medicinal herb. In countries such as Thailand, India, and China it is often used in food.

HEALTH BENEFITS:

Lemongrass oil has antimicrobial, antioxidant, and anti-inflammatory properties.

USES FOR LEMONGRASS

HEALING PROPERTIES:

It is thought that this oil can help calm the senses, reduce stress and anxiety, promote sleep and potentially ease aches and pains. It can also be used as an insect repellent.

HOW TO USE:

As with many of these oils, there are many ways to use them as a spray, for massage, to bathe in, or as a diffuser. The cooling effect of lemongrass is beneficial for the body during hot weather. Use as a topical application with a carrier/base oil.

*If adding essential oil to any product that is intended for the skin, always read the manufacturers instructions, check the amount of essential oils that can be added to the product.